BLIPS ON A SCREEN

Joshua Gage

blips on a screen

©2021 Joshua Gage
All Rights Reserved

First Printing

ISBN 978-1-7350257-1-1

CUTTLEFISH
BOOKS

ACKNOWLEDGEMENTS

Grateful appreciation is offered to the editors and publishers of *Abyss & Apex, Scifaikuest, Star*Line* in which some of these poems have previously appeared or are forthcoming.

blips on a screen

deep space run—
only the lights
from my console

black hole
the pilot drawn to
the absence of stars

twilight—
    the moons we haven't mined
    begin to appear

low Earth orbit
watching the sun rise
somewhere else

quickly one
then another,
these meteors

radio static
the slow pull
of Earthrise

exo-orbit
the pop of my thrusters
running out of fuel

smoking rubble
after the saucers—
wild prairie rose

dust storm
the crater disappears
habitat by habitat

labyrinth walk
the endless blue
of solar panels

first contact
its grey fingers stroke
my hydroponic orchid

from every direction
the skies grow green—
alien armada

Jovian aurora
a hundred colonists
with one expression

Medal of Valor
his textbook salute
with a prosthetic tentacle

Memorial Day
the captured astronaut
sizzles over the coals

lunar prison
after lights out
a transport's contrail

water ration—
the hour between first
and second sunrise

each swig
of my recycled urine
astronomical noon

transit of Venus
a god
in our image?

clawed footprints—
a waning moon
swallows the stars

orbiting alone
the scent of orange blossoms
on the crater's map

uncharted planet—
buried halfway in the dust,
a human skeleton

alien corpse
the scalpel hesitates
just a moment

methane storm---
scientists realign
their specimen jars

research mission—
the winds out there collecting
their own samples

the rover
spreads its solar cells—
strange blue flowers

biennial survey
already covered in blossoms
the last team's habitat

Martian garden
the full stretch
of her tentacle

folding a shirt
the terraformer watches
her last sunrise

space burial
the engine cycles
through our silence

Sapkota crater
the long stretch
of headstone shadows

meteor shower
smoke from a prayer candle
guttering out

green moonlight
the engineer weeps
over a letter from home

Obon Festival
light years away
the smell of fireworks

Christmas Eve
the control panel lights
all we have

nuclear winter
the android's
unfinished sentence

Mare Orientale
the time it takes
for your ashes to scatter

asteroid field
I renew my conversations
with God

abandoned space station
but if you listen
hard enough...

in harmony
with the crescent moon—
bioluminescent scales

hydrating rations—
the glow of the Earth
unblocking the sun

oxygen gone
the taste of promises
I won't keep

reaching the end
of mapped space
the whir of life support

rocket contrails—
all the moons
I'll never visit

twilight
a girl waits at the landing pads
for her father's shuttle

barely snow
my first breath of fresh air
in four years

back at basecamp
the rover's lack of shocks
still in my legs

sleeping quarters
the aliens my daughter fights
with her flashlight

orbiting
the star she wished upon...
sepia portrait

our lives
just blips on a screen
Oranocentric orbit

ABOUT THE AUTHOR

Joshua Gage is an ornery curmudgeon from Cleveland, Ohio. He is a graduate of the Low Residency MFA Program in Creative Writing at Naropa University. He has a penchant for Pendleton shirts, Ethiopian coffee, and any poem strong enough to yank the breath out of his lungs.

www.ingramcontent.com/pod-product-compliance
Lightning Source LLC
Chambersburg PA
CBHW071916070526
44583CB00016B/2013